Into the Rainforest

THIS EDITION
Editorial Management by Oriel Square
Produced for DK by WonderLab Group LLC
Jennifer Emmett, Erica Green, Kate Hale, *Founders*

Editors Grace Hill Smith, Libby Romero, Michaela Weglinski;
Photography Editors Kelley Miller, Annette Kiesow, Nicole DiMella;
Managing Editor Rachel Houghton; **Designers** Project Design Company;
Researcher Michelle Harris; **Copy Editor** Lori Merritt; **Indexer** Connie Binder;
Proofreader Larry Shea; **Reading Specialist** Dr. Jennifer Albro;
Curriculum Specialist Elaine Larson

Published in the United States by DK Publishing
1745 Broadway, 20th Floor, New York, NY 10019

Copyright © 2023 Dorling Kindersley Limited
DK, a Division of Penguin Random House LLC
22 23 24 25 26 10 9 8 7 6 5 4 3 2 1
001-333451-May/2023

All rights reserved.
Without limiting the rights under the copyright reserved above, no part of this publication may be reproduced, stored in or introduced into a retrieval system, or transmitted, in any form, or by any means (electronic, mechanical, photocopying, recording, or otherwise), without the prior written permission of the copyright owner.
Published in Great Britain by Dorling Kindersley Limited

A catalog record for this book
is available from the Library of Congress.
HC ISBN: 978-0-7440-6783-5
PB ISBN: 978-0-7440-6785-9

DK books are available at special discounts when purchased in bulk for sales promotions, premiums, fundraising, or educational use. For details, contact: DK Publishing Special Markets,
1745 Broadway, 20th Floor, New York, NY 10019
SpecialSales@dk.com

Printed and bound in China

The publisher would like to thank the following for their kind permission to reproduce their images:
a=above; c=center; b=below; l=left; r=right; t=top; b/g=background

123RF.com: Rafal Cichawa / rchphoto 4-5, Anan Kaewkhammul / anankkml 16br;
Alamy Stock Photo: imageBROKER / Stefan Huwiler 8-9; **Dorling Kindersley:** Jerry Young 1, 15br;
Dreamstime.com: Andrew Allport 20br, Dirk Ercken / Kikkerdirk 3, 7bc, Christopher Meder 7crb, Ntdanai 7br, Minyun Zhou 12-13bc, 23cl; **Getty Images:** Image Source / Aziz Ary Neto 9br, The Image Bank / John Coletti 9cra;
Getty Images / iStock: DonFord1 4br, 23tl, Moment / Kryssia Campos 9bc, 23cla, Enrico Pescantini 14cb;
Shutterstock.com: Avigator Fortuner 6-7, Tristan Barrington 19bc, Stephane Bidouze 22, BrunoGSMagalhaes 20-21, Jirasak Chuangsen 4c, Det-anan 22clb, Dewin ID 11bl, Sanit Fuangnakhon 11br, Natalia Kuzmina 15cb, Hugh Lansdown 5tc, 21bl, Layue 13br, Anda_Manea 10br, 22bc, NaturesMomentsuk 14-15, Pedro Helder Pinheiro 5br, 16-17, 23clb, Poring Studio 12-13, 22c, Ondrej Prosicky 22cra, Vaclav Sebek 4-5c, 18-19, 23bl, Sekar B 17bc, YAI_SOMKIAT 10-11

Cover images: *Front:* **Dreamstime.com:** Nataliia Darmoroz, SaveJungle b; *Back:* **Dreamstime.com:** Nataliia Darmoroz cra, SaveJungle clb

All other images © Dorling Kindersley
For more information see: www.dkimages.com

For the curious
www.dk.com

Pre-level

Into the Rainforest

Libby Romero

DK

Come with me into this rainforest!

There is rain and mist.

It is warm
and wet here.

tropical rainforest
[TRAA-puh-kul RAYN-faw-ruhst]

There are many trees in this rainforest.
This tree is very tall.

kapok tree
[KAY-paak tree]

There are plants in this rainforest. This plant has big leaves.

leaves

Many plants in this rainforest have flowers. This plant has pink flowers.

orchid
[OR-kuhd]

There are animals here, too.
This sloth lives mainly in the trees.

sloth

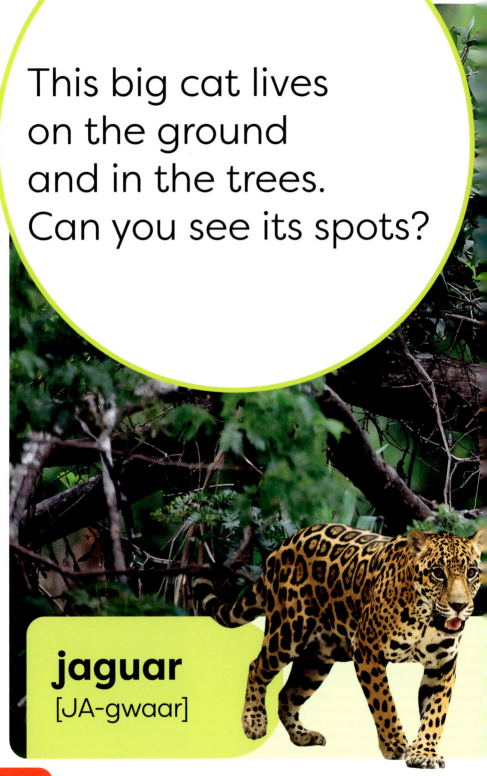

This big cat lives on the ground and in the trees. Can you see its spots?

jaguar
[JA-gwaar]

17

This scaly animal lives near the water. Look at its sharp teeth!

caiman
[KAY-muhn]

This bird flies through the air. It has a bright bill.

toucan
[TOO-kan]

This rainforest is full of life.
It is home for many plants and animals.

Glossary

caiman
an alligator-like animal found in some tropical rainforests

jaguar
a large wild cat found in some tropical rainforests

kapok tree
a very tall tree that grows in tropical rainforests

orchid
a plant with unusual, brightly colored flowers

tropical rainforest
a thick, wet forest that grows in hot places

Quiz

Answer the questions to see what you have learned. Check your answers with an adult.

1. What does it feel like in a tropical rainforest?
2. Which rainforest tree is very tall?
3. Which scaly rainforest animal lives near the water?
4. Which rainforest bird has a bright bill and flies through the air?
5. Which rainforest plant or animal is your favorite? Why?

1. Warm and wet 2. Kapok tree 3. Caiman 4. Toucan
5. Answers will vary